Some bonds are so special,
they become part of your heart...
forever.
I0750707
My Best
Friend
Max
Adventures
with Max

First Edition 2026
Written and illustrated by Paula Bennett
Hartford James LLC
www.hartfordjames.com

ISBN: 979-8-950718-01-4
For permissions or inquiries, contact: **hartfordjamesllc@gmail.com**

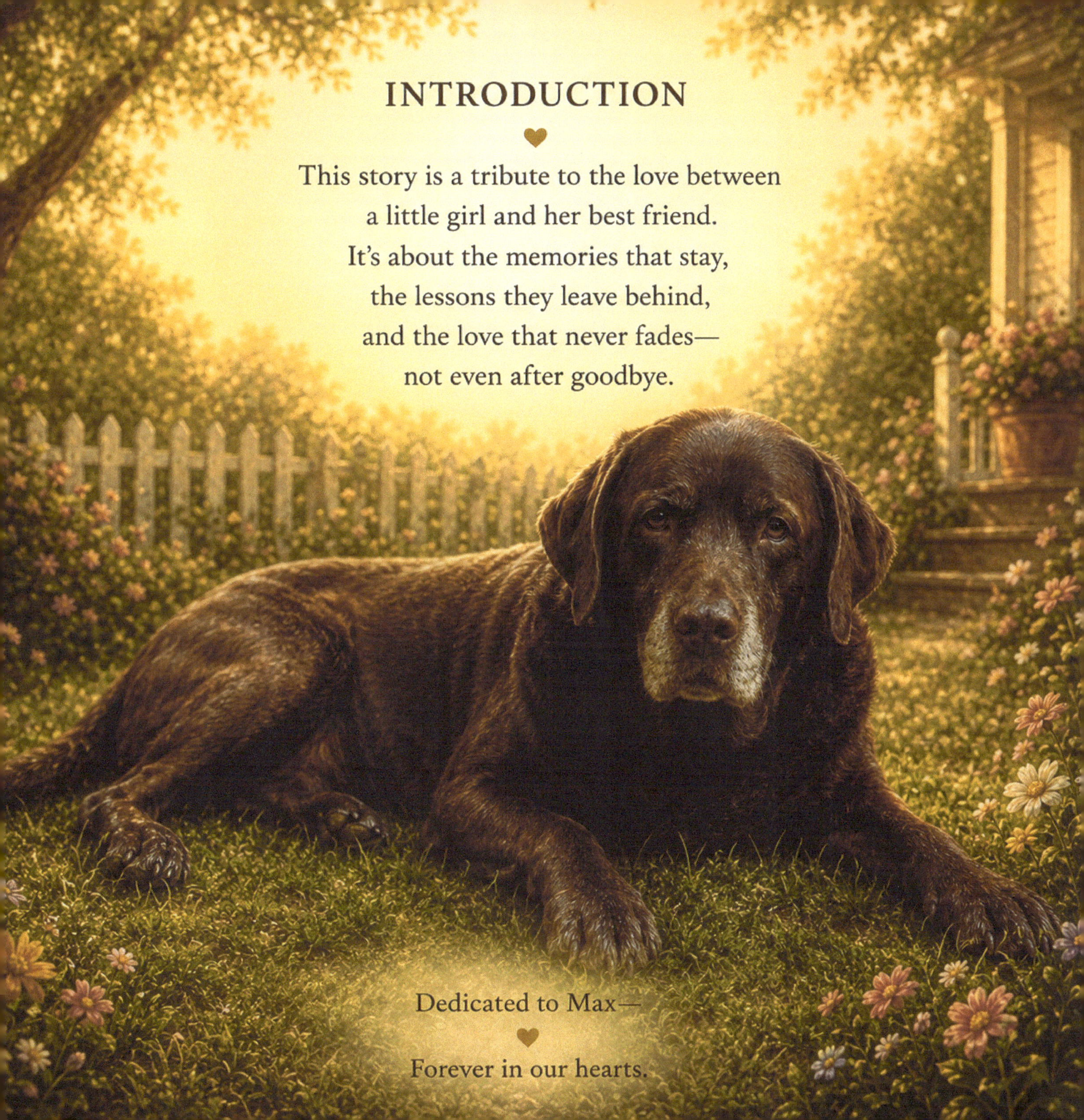

INTRODUCTION

This story is a tribute to the love between
a little girl and her best friend.
It's about the memories that stay,
the lessons they leave behind,
and the love that never fades—
not even after goodbye.

Dedicated to Max—

Forever in our hearts.

Every morning,
Remi looked
for Max.

Max was
always nearby.

They ate breakfast together every day.

Max followed
Remi everywhere.

"Let's go outside
and play ball!"
said Remi.

Max always
watched over her.

One afternoon,
dark clouds
filled the sky.

But
Max stayed close.

Soon, they fell
asleep together.

After their nap, Remi
read stories to Max.
Bedtime
Tales
Sweet Dreams
Little Star
Good Night, Little One

But one day,
Max moved a little slower.

His face was
turning gray too.

"Are you getting old?"
Remi whispered.

Gammy smiled softly.
"Sometimes
best friends
grow old."

So Remi
stayed close to Max.

"You are my
best friend forever,"
Remi said.

One quiet day,
Remi told Max goodbye.

Remi missed
Max very much.

But together, they remembered all the happy days.
My Best Friend

and Max
That night, Remi gazed at the stars and whispered, “I know you’re safe, Max.”
Best Friends Forever

Before bed, Remi whispered, "Goodnight, Max. I love you, and you will always be in my heart." And deep inside her heart, Max was still there.

Max ♡
The best friend anyone could have.
Loyal, soft, gentle, patient
and always by your side
happy or sad.
Waited for you always.
He will forever be missed.
He lived
14.5 years
on this earth.
Now he is in heaven
with his beloved brother
Zeus ♡
Running in the fields,
playing ball,
free and happy,
together again.
Love never leaves. ♥ Forever in our hearts.

Loyal to the end.
Gentle. Steady.
Always by my side.
Forever in my heart.

DECEMBER 2011 ~ MAY 2026

And somehow, when
the world was quiet...
Remi still felt Max
beside her.

www.ingramcontent.com/pod-product-compliance
Lightning Source LLC
LaVergne TN
LVHW070207110826
845147LV00002B/521

* 9 7 9 8 9 5 0 7 1 8 0 1 4 *